METEOR SHOWERS

Marne Ventura

childsworld.com

Published by The Child's World®
800-599-READ • www.childsworld.com

Copyright © 2025 by The Child's World®
All rights reserved. No part of this book may be reproduced or utilized in any form or by any means without written permission from the publisher.

Photography Credits
Photographs ©: Shutterstock Images, cover, 1, 5, 8, 13 (meteors); Ingo Bartussek/Shutterstock Images, 2–3; Bill Ingalls/NASA, 6; iStockphoto, 9; Dan Burbank/NASA, 11; Gerald Rhemann, 12; Giotto Project/ESA/NASA, 13 (comet); NASA, 13 (Earth), 13 (Sun); Gilberto Souza/Shutterstock Images, 15; Tatyana Tomsickova/iStockphoto, 17; Ashley Hampson/iStockphoto, 18; Brian Spencer/Shutterstock Images, 20

ISBN Information
9781503894426 (Reinforced Library Binding)
9781503895164 (Portable Document Format)
9781503895980 (Online Multi-user eBook)
9781503896802 (Electronic Publication)

LCCN 2024941364

Printed in the United States of America

ABOUT THE AUTHOR

Marne Ventura is the author of more than 150 books for children. She holds a master's degree in education from the University of California. She enjoys writing about STEM, arts and crafts, finance, people and places, food, and careers. Ventura and her family live in California.

CONTENTS

CHAPTER ONE
WAKE UP! . . . 4

CHAPTER TWO
THE SCIENCE BEHIND METEOR SHOWERS . . . 10

CHAPTER THREE
WHERE TO SEE A METEOR SHOWER . . . 16

Glossary . . . 22
Fast Facts . . . 23
One Stride Further . . . 23
Find Out More . . . 24
Index . . . 24

CHAPTER ONE

WAKE UP!

"Wake up! It's happening!" Antonio's sister stood next to his bed. "Let's go! Everyone's out back."

Antonio rolled over and looked at the clock. It was 2 a.m. He threw back the covers and followed Bella to the backyard. Grandma, Grandpa, Mom, and Dad sat in lawn chairs on the patio.

"Look over there!" Grandpa said, pointing to the northeastern sky. Grandma spread out a quilt on the grass. Antonio lay on his back and searched the dark sky.

At first, Antonio just saw stars. Some were pinpoints of light. Others were big and bright. Then a streak of light shot across the darkness and disappeared. It was a meteor! Another one followed. Then another shot across the sky in the opposite direction. The longer he watched, the more streaks of light Antonio saw. At times, there were so many that they looked like faraway fireworks.

"It's so beautiful!" Bella said.

For better chances of seeing a meteor shower, experts recommend that people spend at least an hour outside to let their eyes adjust to the darkness. They should not use devices with screens, as this can make it harder for their eyes to adjust.

Meteors can have long tails.

Antonio agreed. Every August, he and his family visited his grandparents in the Southern California desert. Away from the city lights, the dark sky was perfect for watching meteor showers. It was fun to be outside in the middle of the night. All year long, Antonio looked forward to the warm desert air and the amazing light show.

A meteor is a space rock that has entered Earth's **atmosphere**. The space rock falls through the sky toward Earth. As it falls, a bright streak of light trails behind it. The streak of light is caused as the meteor burns up in Earth's atmosphere. People who see this **phenomenon** often call it a "shooting star." A meteor shower occurs when multiple meteors streak through the sky during a short period of time.

CONSTELLATIONS

Stargazers in ancient cultures noticed that groups of stars formed patterns. They gave these patterns names based on the shapes they created. For example, lines drawn between the North Star and nearby stars look like the handle of a ladle. This constellation became known as the Little Dipper. Because constellations stayed in place in the sky, people used them as landmarks. Over time, people have continued to name constellations. Today there are 88 official constellations.

LITTLE DIPPER

BIG DIPPER

A meteor can appear at any time. But the major meteor showers happen around the same time every year. Some have been occurring for hundreds of years. A meteor shower is named for the constellation where it appears to originate. Showers happen on a consistent, predictable schedule. Antonio and his family watched the Perseid (PUR-see-id) meteor shower. The streaks of light all seemed to come from the constellation Perseus. The Perseid meteor shower happens every August. Sightings of Perseids go back a long time. Chinese records from 2,000 years ago made note of the shower.

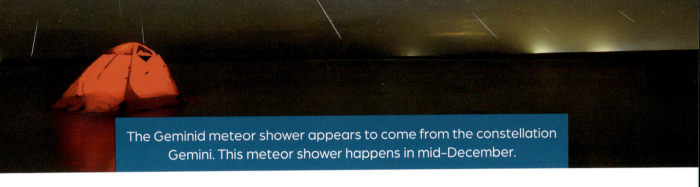

The Geminid meteor shower appears to come from the constellation Gemini. This meteor shower happens in mid-December.

Almost 1,000 possible meteor showers have been reported to the International Astronomical Union. Only around 100 are established. An established meteor shower has a known cause and appears on a consistent schedule. When scientists know what causes a certain meteor shower, they can predict when it will happen.

CHAPTER TWO

THE SCIENCE BEHIND METEOR SHOWERS

Meteor showers are caused by space **debris**. Asteroids can create this debris. But most meteor showers happen when Earth passes through the **orbit** of a comet. Comets are large objects made of rock, dust, and ice. Like Earth, comets orbit the Sun. But comet orbits are larger than Earth's orbit. They are also more oval shaped. Comets travel to the distant edges of the solar system. They take a long time to complete an orbit around the sun. As a comet gets close to the Sun, the comet heats up. Its icy surface boils off. The comet leaves tails of dust and gas. The dust tail is made of tiny **particles** of rock. Earth can pass through the comet's dust tail. Then the rocky debris enters Earth's atmosphere. When that happens, these bits of rocky debris become meteors.

An astronaut in orbit took this photo of Comet Lovejoy when it was visible from Earth in 2011.

Comets are often named for the people who discover them. Lewis Swift and Horace Tuttle each discovered Comet Swift-Tuttle in 1862, which is why it is named after both of them.

A comet's orbit is predictable, like Earth's. This is how scientists know when certain meteor showers will happen. For example, the Perseid meteor shower is caused by debris from Comet Swift-Tuttle. Earth passes through Swift-Tuttle's orbit at the same time each year. This is why Perseids peak in August. The Orionid meteor shower takes place every October. This is when Earth crosses the orbit of Halley's comet.

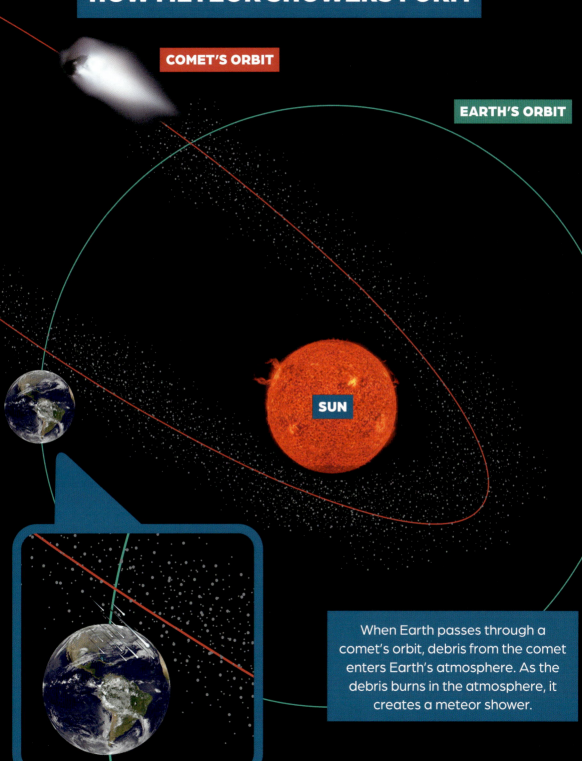

Meteors that enter Earth's atmosphere are moving at high speeds. The fastest travel at speeds of 44 miles per second (71 kps). As a meteor speeds through the gases of Earth's atmosphere, it creates friction. Friction is the result of one object rubbing against another. Both the gases and the meteor are made of **molecules**. Friction makes molecules move faster. This gives them more energy. The energy makes heat. This heat usually burns up the meteor. The gases around the meteor glow. The bright streak of light that trails behind a meteor is what sky-watchers see when a meteor heats up and is burned away.

Meteors that fall toward Earth during showers usually do not reach the ground. Many are as small as a grain of sand. The material they are made of is **fragile**. For this reason, most completely burn up in the atmosphere.

METEOROID, METEOR, METEORITE

Planets and comets are not the only objects in the solar system that orbit the Sun. Asteroids are objects that range in size from 329 miles (530 km) across to under 33 feet (10 m). They are made of rock, clay, iron, and nickel. Comets are made of dust, rock, and ice. A small piece of an asteroid or comet is called a meteoroid. When it enters Earth's atmosphere, it becomes a meteor. If it makes it through the atmosphere to hit the ground, it is called a meteorite.

Scientists say about 48.5 tons (44 mt) of meteoric material falls toward Earth every day. Almost all of it is burned away by Earth's atmosphere.

What a meteor is made of affects how it looks. People have seen meteors with red, yellow, or green tails. The tail color is caused by a chemical reaction in the meteor's molecules. For example, meteors made of calcium give off a purple color when they burn. Meteors made of magnesium have green or teal tails. The speed of the meteor determines its color as well. Faster-moving meteors have the brightest tails.

CHAPTER THREE

WHERE TO SEE A METEOR SHOWER

All the meteors in a shower look as if they come from the same place in the sky. This place is called the radiant. A meteor shower is named after the constellation in which its radiant lies. Scientists know the meteors do not actually come from the constellations. But constellations help sky-watchers know where to look to see a meteor shower.

Since Earth passes through the same orbit each year, scientists can predict when the major meteor showers will happen. Different space agencies post meteor shower calendars. These can be found online. American Meteor Society, EarthSky, and the Old Farmer's Almanac are sources for calendars. So is Space.com.

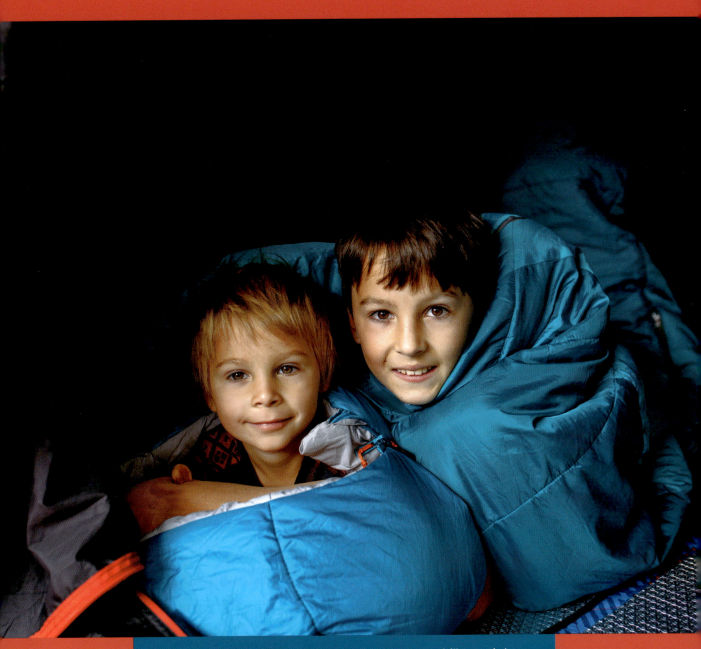

Even during the summer, weather can get chilly at night. Experts recommend that sky-watchers dress warmly and make themselves comfortable when watching a meteor shower.

The first recorded sighting of the Lyrid meteor shower was in 687 BC.

There are a few things sky-watchers can do to increase their chances of seeing a good show. One is to find out the peak time for the shower. This is when it will be easiest to see a lot of meteors. Peak time is posted on most meteor shower calendars. It also helps to find a dark place away from city lights. If the moon is full or bright, people will have a harder time seeing meteors. And finally, patience is important! Meteor showers do not always have constant activity. Sometimes there are long periods between meteors. Experts recommend watching for at least an hour.

The number of meteors that sky-watchers can see during a meteor shower varies. It depends on the meteor shower, the weather, and the sky conditions. On a clear night, they might see one per minute. The American Meteor Society reports that the Taurid and April Lyrid meteor showers have about 10 to 15 meteors per hour. Perseids or Geminids can have 50 to 100 meteors per hour. Meteor showers can last from a few hours to a few nights.

People around the world may be lucky enough to see a meteor shower.

People have been watching meteor showers for thousands of years. Before modern science, many cultures explained meteor showers with myths and legends. Some said meteors were sent by the gods as a sign or warning. Some described shooting stars as tears of a **saint** falling from the sky. Throughout history, meteor showers have provided people with spectacular light shows. Sky-watchers do not need any special equipment to enjoy the beauty. People of all ages, around the world, have the chance to see a meteor shower every year.

METEOR SUPERSTITIONS

Many cultures have **superstitions** associated with meteors. One common superstition is wishing on shooting stars. Many people see meteors as signs of luck or good fortune. In some cultures, meteors are associated with the afterlife. People see them as signs from loved ones. But some cultures have negative superstitions. They see meteors as signs of bad fortune.

GLOSSARY

atmosphere (AT-muss-feer) An atmosphere is the layer of gases that surrounds a planet. Meteor showers happen when space debris burns up in Earth's atmosphere.

debris (duh-BREE) Debris is made up of pieces of things that have been destroyed or broken down. A comet leaves a trail of rocky debris in its orbit.

fragile (FRA-juhl) Something fragile is easily broken. Most meteors are small and fragile.

molecules (MAH-luh-kyools) Molecules are the smallest parts of a substance. Meteors are made up of molecules.

orbit (OR-bit) An orbit is the rounded path that an object takes as it goes around a larger object. Earth's orbit around the Sun is much smaller than a comet's orbit around the Sun.

particles (PAR-tih-kullz) Particles are tiny parts of something. Comets give off particles of ice and dust.

phenomenon (fuh-NAH-muh-nahn) A phenomenon is an observable event that can be explained by science. A meteor shower is an amazing phenomenon.

saint (SAYNT) A saint is a holy person. One superstition says meteor showers are the tears of a saint.

superstitions (soo-pur-STIH-shuhnz) Superstitions are beliefs that certain events cause good or bad luck. There are many superstitions about meteors, such as wishing on a shooting star.

FAST FACTS

✳ A meteor is a space rock that has entered Earth's atmosphere.

✳ Meteors look like streaks of light in the night sky.

✳ Meteor showers are named for the constellations where they seem to originate.

✳ Meteor showers happen when Earth passes through space debris. This debris often comes from comets.

✳ Comets are space objects made from rock, dust, and ice. When a comet gets close to the Sun, its icy surface boils off. The comet leaves a gas tail and a dust tail.

✳ Debris from the comet enters Earth's atmosphere. Friction causes it to burn up, which causes a streak of light known as a meteor.

✳ Scientists can predict when meteor showers will occur.

✳ Space agencies post calendars of meteor showers.

✳ A dark sky away from city lights is the best location to see meteor showers.

ONE STRIDE FURTHER

✳ What skills do you think a scientist who studies meteors would need?

✳ Would you be interested in studying meteors? Why or why not?

✳ Why do you think people make wishes when they see meteors?

FIND OUT MORE

IN THE LIBRARY

Kruesi, Liz. *Space*. Parker, CO: The Child's World, 2021.

Regas, Dean. *1,000 Facts About Space*. Washington, DC: National Geographic Kids, 2022.

Ringstad, Arnold. *Asteroids, Meteorites, and Comets*. Parker, CO: The Child's World, 2021.

ON THE WEB

Visit our website for links about meteor showers:

childsworld.com/links

Note to Parents, Caregivers, Teachers, and Librarians: We routinely verify our web links to make sure they are safe and active sites. So encourage your readers to check them out!

INDEX

April Lyrids, 19
asteroids, 10, 14

calendars, 16–19
causes, 7, 9, 10–15
colors, 15
Comet Swift-Tuttle, 12
comets, 10–12, 13, 14
constellations, 8, 16

debris, 7, 10–14

Geminids, 19

Halley's comet, 12

International Astronomical Union, 9

meteorites, 14
meteoroids, 14

Orionids, 12

Perseids, 8, 12, 19

radiants, 8, 16

speed, 14–15
superstitions, 21

Taurids, 19
tips for viewing, 7, 16–19